This book belongs to
S. Rogers

A First-Start Easy Reader

This easy reader contains only 33 different words,
repeated often to help the young reader develop
word recognition and interest in reading.

Basic word list for *Happy Jack*

got	job	Jack
a	were	Millie
was	some	Jo
and	soup	Flo
too	taste	Aunt
the	said	hungry
let	over	wanted
me	cake	dropped
all	pie	spilled
not	they	happy
new	still	waiter

Happy Jack

Written by Sharon Peters

Illustrated by Paul Harvey

Troll Associates

ISBN 0-89375-280-0

Jack got a new job.

Jack was a waiter.

Aunt Millie, Aunt Jo and Aunt Flo
were hungry.

Jack was hungry, too.

Aunt Millie wanted some soup.

"OH, WAITER."

Jack got the soup.

"Let me taste the soup," said Jack.

Jack dropped the soup.

Jack spilled the soup—

all over Aunt Millie.

Aunt Millie was not happy.

Aunt Jo wanted some cake.

Jack got the cake.

"Let me taste the cake," said Jack.

Jack dropped the cake.

Jack spilled the cake—

all over Aunt Jo.

Aunt Jo was not happy.

Jack got the pie.

"Let me taste the pie," said Jack.

Jack dropped the pie.

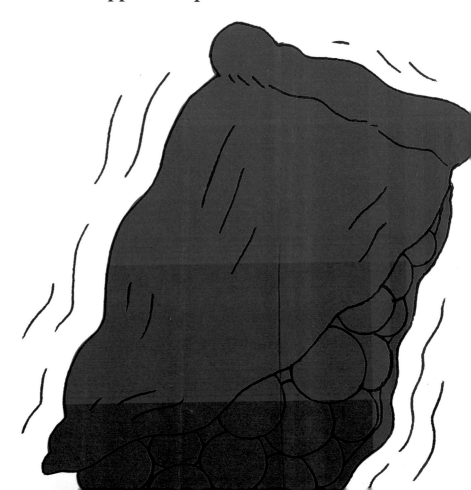

Jack spilled the pie—
all over Aunt Flo.

Aunt Flo was not happy.

Aunt Millie, Aunt Jo and Aunt Flo
were not happy.

They were still hungry.

Jack was hungry, too.

Jack got a new job.

Aunt Flo, Aunt Millie and Aunt Jo
were happy.